Lord I'm afraid

Roger Campbell

CHRISTIAN LITERATURE CRUSADE
Fort Washington, Pennsylvania 19034

CHRISTIAN LITERATURE CRUSADE
Fort Washington, Pennsylvania 19034

CANADA
Elgin, Ontario K0G 1E0

GREAT BRITAIN
The Dean, Alresford, Hampshire

AUSTRALIA
P.O. Box 91, Pennant Hills, N.S.W. 2120

Copyright©1980
Christian Literature Crusade, Inc.
Fort Washington, Pennsylvania, U.S.A.

ISBN 0-87508-056-1

Printed in the United States of America

TO DAVID
MY SON

INTRODUCTION

When God called Adam from hiding, after the fall, he answered, "I heard thy voice in the garden, and I was afraid" (Genesis 3:10). Fear has kept people hiding through the ages.

Fear is a monster that stalks us all. It brings depression, stifles ability, drains energy, diminishes courage, and robs life of adventure and success.

Some fears are real and others are imaginary. Who has not been troubled by some supposed impending tragedy that never happened? In those cases, we are relieved to have escaped unharmed. But have we? Who can tell the impact on bodies and minds during the time of waiting in fear?

For more than twenty years my work as a minister has brought me into contact with people in the crisis times of their lives. I have been there when the worst seemed likely. These experiences have taught me that the promises of the Bible provide the best defense against fear. Faith grows as a result of exposure to the Bible: "So, then, faith cometh by hearing, and hearing by the word of God" (Romans 10:17). And faith overcomes fear.

It would be less than honest to leave the impression that the pages that follow only describe the fears of others. Fear has been my companion too often. Ministers are not immune to fear. Nevertheless, in my trembling times, I have gone to the Bible to find help. It is a source of strength that does not fail.

"I sought the LORD, and he heard me, and delivered me from all my fears" (Psalm 34:4).

Roger F. Campbell

THE DAY

Lord,
I'm afraid
   of the day.
Who knows
   what a day
     may bring forth?
Sounds Biblical.
Does that mean
   the worst
   is likely?
Am I up to the day?

As thy days, so shall thy strength be.
        Deuteronomy 33:25

BELIEVING
Lord,
I'm afraid
   to believe.
Unbelief parades
   theories
      degrees
         acceptance.
Ancient bones
Carbon dating
Learned lectures.
What is truth?

Thy word is truth.
                 John 17:17
Heaven and earth shall pass away, but my
words shall not pass away.
                 Matthew 24:35

STORMS

Lord,
I'm afraid
   of storms.
Clouds stampeding.
Lightning
   splitting the darkness.
Winds
   announcing destruction.
Omnipotence
   poised for judgment.
Where shall I hide?

And a man shall be like an hiding place
from the wind, and a covert from the
tempest; like rivers of water in a dry place,
like the shadow of a great rock in a weary
land.

Isaiah 32:2

FORGIVENESS

Lord,
I'm afraid
    You're tired of me.
I'm back again
Confessing the same sin.
I meant well
    but fell.
Can you forgive me again?
And again?

If we confess our sins, he is faithful and just
to forgive us our sins, and to cleanse us
from all unrighteousness.
                       1 John 1:9

WAITING

Lord,
I'm afraid
    something has happened.
I've walked miles
    wondering
        worrying.
So many dangers out there
    drunks
    criminals.
What can I do from here?

Casting all your care upon him; for he
careth for you.

                1Peter 5:7

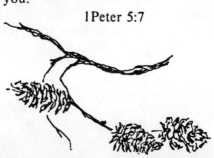

THE MAILMAN

Lord,
I'm afraid
    of the mailman.
He specializes
    in bills
    and bad news.
Junk mail
    would be welcome.
It's painless.
Do you have any good news?

The Spirit of the Lord God is upon me,
because the LORD hath anointed me to
preach good tidings unto the meek; he hath
sent me to bind up the brokenhearted, to
proclaim liberty to the captives, and the
opening of the prison to those who are
bound.

                Isaiah 61:1

THE CHURCH

Lord,
I'm afraid
for my church.
Life is lacking
And love
is absent too.
We go through the motions
But something is missing.
Is there a prescription
for a sick church?

And be not drunk with wine, in which is
excess, but be filled with the Spirit.
Ephesians 5:18

MY COUNTRY

Lord,
I'm afraid
    for my country.
Heaven's view
    must be appalling.
Lust is king
Booze
    second in command.
Money
    occupies the temple.
Justice falters.
Babies
    refused life.
And for mercy's sake
    the old and ill
    are offered death.
Is there healing
    for the land?

If my people, who are called by my name,
shall humble themselves, and pray, and seek
my face, and turn from their wicked ways,
then will I hear from heaven, and will
forgive their sin, and will heal their land.
                    2 Chronicles 7:14

GETTING OLDER

Lord,
I'm afraid
   to grow old.
Everything is changing
   except the countdown.
Days are longer
Years shorter
   like my breath.
What will become of me
   when I'm old?

And even to your old age I am he; and even
to gray hairs will I carry you; I have made,
and I will bear; even I will carry, and will
deliver you.

Isaiah 46:4

TRAVELING

Lord,
I'm afraid
    to travel.
Death
    drives the highways.
There's so much
    I'd like to see.
Friends
    I long to meet.
But is it safe to travel?

The horse is prepared for the day of battle,
but safety is from the LORD.
                Proverbs 21:31

LOVE

Lord,
I'm afraid
   to love.
Hearts are fragile
And mine
   has been broken.
Shall I invest
   my love again?

To everything there is a season, and a time
to every purpose under the heaven: A time
to love.

Ecclesiastes 3:1,8

FLYING

Lord,
I'm afraid
     to fly.
An earthling‾
     is what I am.
Security
     takes flight
     at the take-off.
My flight is boarding
But is air enough
               underneath?

The eternal God is thy refuge, and
underneath are the everlasting arms.
Deuteronomy 33:27

MARRIAGE

Lord,
I'm afraid
    to marry.
I need love
But
    is marriage
    that important?
Can we be closer
    than we are now?

Therefore shall a man leave his father and
his mother, and shall cleave unto his wife;
and they shall be one flesh.

                      Genesis 2:24

CHILDREN

Lord,
I'm afraid
    to have children.
The world
    is evil.
Times
    are uncertain.
Communism threatens.
War seems imminent.
Crime runs rampant.
Why bring children
    into a world like this?

Lo, children are an heritage from the Lord;
and the fruit of the womb is his reward.
Psalm 127:3

GROWN CHILDREN

Lord,
I'm afraid
    for my children.
When they left
Concern stayed.
I long to
    tuck them in.
Know they're safe.
Will You care for them
    as You did for me?

Thy faithfulness is unto all generations.
Psalm 119:90

SINGLE

Lord,
I'm afraid
 I'll not marry.
The years
 are getting away
 like my prospects.
Friends
 have found love.
Some
 have loved
 and lost.
I'm still single.
Can that be
 in Your will?

Brethren, let every man, in whatever state he
is called, there abide with God.
 1 Corinthians 7:24

THE DARK

Lord,
I'm afraid
   of the dark.
Since childhood
   the darkness
   has ruled me.
Some experience
   left its mark.
What can I do
   about being afraid
   when the lights go out?

Yea, the darkness hideth not from thee, but
the night shineth as the day; the darkness
and the light are both alike to thee.
                     Psalm 139:12

HEALTH

Lord,
I'm afraid
   my health is gone.
I feel strange
   tired
      weak
         hurting.
Scary sensations.
The doctor?
   Avoided.
Fearing
   what he may find.
Have I waited too long?

Behold, I am the LORD, the God of all
flesh; is there anything too hard for me?
                Jeremiah 32:27

WORDS

Lord,
I'm afraid
    I've said the wrong thing.
Bombed.
I can't forget that look...
        surprised
            disappointed
                wounded.
Who repairs
        bad sentence construction?

Therefore, if thou bring thy gift to the altar,
and there rememberest that thy brother hath
anything against thee, leave there thy gift
before the altar and go thy way; first be
reconciled to thy brother, and then come
and offer thy gift.

                    Matthew 5:23-24

REJECTION

Lord,
I'm afraid
    of rejection.
Acceptance
    means everything.
Approval
    is my goal.
Others form my convictions.
The crowd
    makes my decisions.
If I do right
    will anyone accept me?

He hath made us accepted in the Beloved.
                Ephesians 1:6

REJOICING

Lord,
I'm afraid
    to rejoice.
Even when all is well
I ask:
    Can this last?
On mountaintops
    the view is lost
        for fear of falling.
Is it safe
    to rejoice
        in Your love?

Rejoice in the Lord always; and again I say,
Rejoice.
                Philippians 4:4

PEOPLE

Lord,
I'm afraid
    of people.
I feel so inferior.
And if I speak
    will they listen?
Who am I?

Be not afraid of their faces; for I am with
thee to deliver thee, saith the LORD.
                        Jeremiah 1:8

SURRENDER

Lord,
I'm afraid
    to surrender.
"Not my will"
    is difficult
        to pray.
I've built my castles
    charted my course
    set my goals.
Is surrender
    always
        unconditional?

He that loveth father or mother more than
me, is not worthy of me; and he that loveth
son or daughter more than me, is not
worthy of me. And he that taketh not his
cross and followeth after me, is not worthy
of me.

Matthew 10:37-38

GIVING

Lord,
I'm afraid
    to give.
Tomorrow
    holds no guarantees.
If I give
    my nest egg
What will I do
    on rainy days?

Give, and it shall be given unto you; good
measure, pressed down, and shaken
together, and running over, shall men give
into your bosom. For with the same
measure that ye measure it shall be
measured to you again.

Luke 6:38

CONFESSING CHRIST
Lord,
I'm afraid
    to declare my faith.
You know me.
I'm quiet
    private
        reserved
            not pushy.
So what do You expect?

Whosoever, therefore, shall confess me
before men, him will I confess also before
my Father, who is in heaven.
                    Matthew 10:32

WITNESSING
Lord,
I'm afraid
   to witness.
Everyone
   seems unapproachable.
Is it right
   to intrude
      unwanted?
And my pastor,
What will he do?

He that goeth forth and weepeth, bearing
precious seed, shall doubtless come again
with rejoicing, bringing his sheaves with
him.
                    Psalm 126:6
If I will that he tarry till I come, what is
that to thee? Follow thou me.
                    John 21:22

THE MISSION FIELD
Lord,
I'm afraid to go
    to the mission field.
Nobody
    knows my fear.
Here I am
    ready to depart.
And terrified.
Deputation was difficult
But friendly faces
    kept me going.
What will I do
Alone in a strange land?

Lo, I am with you always, even unto the
end of the age.

Matthew 28:20

TEACHING

Lord,
I'm afraid
    to teach my class.
Here I am
    untrained
        inexperienced
        petrified.
How did I get into this?
What can I say?

Who hath made man's mouth? Or who
maketh the dumb, or deaf, or the seeing, or
the blind? Have not I, the LORD? Now
therefore go, and I will be with thy mouth
and teach thee what thou shalt say.
                Exodus 4:11-12

DISCARDED DREAM
Lord,
I'm afraid
    to fulfill my dream.
It's risky.
I'm successful.
I'm secure.
I'm comfortable
I'm getting older.
Others won't understand.
Does it matter?

But without faith it is impossible to please
him.
                Hebrews 11:6
For whatever is not of faith is sin.
                Romans 14:23

MOVING

Lord,
I'm afraid
   to move.
I don't know anyone
            there.
I'll be lonely
            there.
I won't like it
            there.
Are You going along?

Have not I commanded thee? Be strong and
of good courage; be not afraid, neither be
thou dismayed; for the LORD thy God is
with thee wherever thou goest.

Joshua 1:9

DECISIONS

Lord,
I'm afraid
        to make decisions.
Floating
        decreases responsibility.
In neutral
        I'm not to blame.
Coasting
        saves energy.
But in not deciding
        I decide.
What shall I do?

Trust in the Lord with all thine heart, and
lean not unto thine own understanding. In
all thy ways acknowledge him, and he shall
direct thy paths.

                    Proverbs 3:5-6

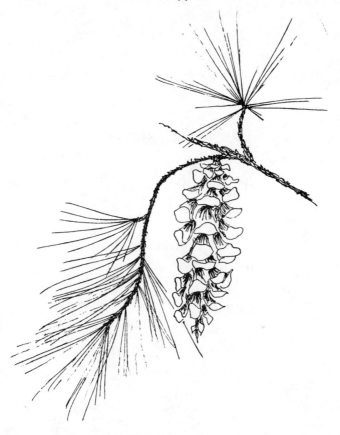

LOCKING UP

Lord,
I'm afraid
    I didn't lock up.
I remember locking.
But when?
Is that click
    the sound of security
    or wishful thinking?
Shall I fly home
    and lock the door?

Except the LORD build the house, they
labor in vain that build it; except the LORD
keep the city, the watchman waketh but in
vain.

Psalm 127:1

LOSING FRIENDS
Lord,
I'm afraid
    of losing friends.
They're acting distant
            cool
                aloof.
Do they believe
        Mrs. Loosetongue?
Will I be alone?

There is a friend who sticketh closer than a
brother.
                    Proverbs 18:24
I will never leave thee, nor forsake thee.
                    Hebrews 13:5

EATING

Lord,
I'm afraid
   to eat.
What about
   additives
      chemicals
         impurities?
And who knows
   how clean the kitchen?
If I consume
Will I be consumed?

There is nothing from outside of a man that,
entering into him, can defile him; but the
things which come out of him, those are
they that defile the man.

                    Mark 7:15

THE HOSPITAL
Lord,
I'm afraid
    to go to the hospital.
Some never return.
And the tales
    of Mrs. Love-to-be-sick
    keep coming to mind.
Tests
Tubes
Needles
And everything white.
Is this the end?

He shall call upon me, and I will answer
him. I will be with him in trouble; I will
deliver him, and honor him. With long life
will I satisfy him, and show him my
salvation.

Psalm 91:15-16

INTENSIVE CARE
Lord,
I'm afraid
he'll die.
This waiting room
intensifies fear.
Five minutes hourly
And all that equipment.
Is there any hope?

Call unto me, and I will answer thee, and
show thee great and mighty things, which
thou knowest not.

Jeremiah 33:3

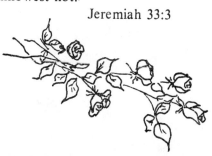

DEATH

Lord,
I'm afraid
    to die.
I like certainties:
This room
My bed
Sunlight
Warmth
Family
Friends
Sight
Breath.
What's out there?

For to me to live is Christ, and to die is
gain.
                    Philippians 1:21
We are confident, I say, and willing rather
to be absent from the body, and to be
present with the Lord.
                    2 Corinthians 5:8

THE TELEPHONE
Lord,
I'm afraid
    of the telephone.
Unwanted words
        may dwell
        at the bell.
My hand withdraws
    from bad news.
A friendly call
Would be welcome.
But is it worth the risk?

Be not afraid of sudden fear.
                Proverbs 3:25
Be of good cheer; it is I; be not afraid.
                Matthew 14:27

BACKSLIDING

Lord,
I'm afraid
    I'm backsliding.
I feel it
    in my knees.
Prayer
    has become routine.
Bible study
    is only a duty.
Church attendance
    is unaffected
    but ineffectual.
Dedication
    is declining.
What's the route
    back to blessing?

Remember, therefore, from where thou art
fallen, and repent, and do the first works.
Revelation 2:5

THE DEVIL

Lord,
I'm afraid
    of the devil.
A roaring lion
    is no joke.
An angel of light
    is a deceiver.
An accuser
    I don't need.
How can I overcome
    so powerful
    an enemy?

Ye are of God, little children, and have
overcome them, because greater is he that is
in you, than he that is in the world.

1 John 4:4

TEMPTATION
Lord,
I'm afraid
of temptation.
The pull
seems irresistible.
All I love
could be lost.
My future
is on the line.
Is it possible to resist
every time?

There hath no temptation taken you but
such as is common to man; but God is
faithful, who will not permit you to be
tempted above that ye are able, but will,
with the temptation, also make the way to
escape, that ye may be able to bear it.
1 Corinthians 10:13

LOSS OF JOB

Lord,
I'm afraid
        I'll lose my job.
My boss
        is avoiding me.
The economy
        is wobbly.
The warehouse
        is filling up.
And the day isn't.
I may be unemployed
                        tomorrow.
Any suggestions?

Be, therefore, not anxious about tomorrow;
for tomorrow will be anxious for the things
of itself.
                        Matthew 6:34

MONEY TROUBLE
Lord,
I'm afraid
    of bankruptcy.
My job is shaky.
The forecasters
    missed this slump.
Are they in debt?
And there's my age.
Do You have any resources
    I haven't listed?

But my God shall supply all your need
according to his riches in glory by Christ
Jesus.

Philippians 4:19

HOMELESS

Lord,
I'm afraid
   we'll lose our home.
Our income
   is losing
   to the outgo.
And it's winter.
Do You know
   how it feels
   to be homeless?

And Jesus saith unto him, The foxes have
holes, and the birds of the air have nests,
but the Son of man hath not where to lay
his head.

Matthew 8:20

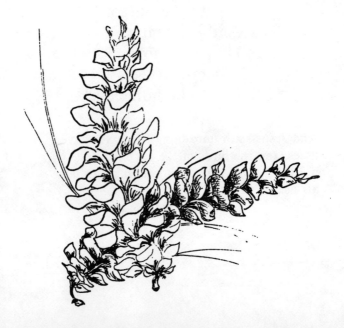

FAILURE

Lord,
I'm afraid
    of failure.
Opportunity knocks.
The possibilities
    seem unlimited
The challenge
    breathtaking.
But should I leave
    a sure thing?

By faith Abraham, when he was called to go
out into a place which he should after
receive for an inheritance, obeyed; and he
went out, not knowing where he went.
Hebrews 11:8

NEW JOB

Lord,
I'm afraid
of this new job.
Was it a mistake
to accept this position?
My old job
was a breeze.
I could work
with my eyes closed
and my brain in neutral.
Can I make it here?

I can do all things through Christ, who
strengtheneth me.
Philippians 4:13

SLEEP

Lord,
I'm afraid
      to sleep.
Falling eyelids
      seem so final.
Will I awake?
And about tomorrow,
Is it worth waking for?

It is vain for you to rise up early, to sit up
late, to eat the bread of sorrows; for so he
giveth his beloved sleep.

                              Psalm 127:2

SPECIAL PROBLEMS
Lord,
I'm afraid
    I can't hold up.
Others are watching.
I need to be strong.
But these problems
    are overwhelming
The situation
    totally unexpected.
Do you have a promise
    for fainting days?

When thou passest through the waters, I will
be with thee; and through the rivers, they
shall not overflow thee; when thou walkest
through the fire, thou shalt not be burned,
neither shall the flame kindle upon thee.

Isaiah 43:2

WORLD CONDITIONS
Lord,
I'm afraid
of world conditions.
Pollution
Overpopulation
Violence
Earthquakes
Famines
Weather changes
Middle East
Energy shortage
Space travel
Computers
666
What next?

And when these things begin to come to
pass, then look up, and lift up your heads;
for your redemption draweth near.
Luke 21:28

THE FUTURE

Lord,
I'm afraid
of the future.
Is it wrong
to long
for a preview?
Doomsayers threaten.
Are they right?
And Your people,
What will they do
when trouble comes?

For I am persuaded that neither death, nor
life, nor angels, nor principalities, nor
powers, nor things present, nor things to
come, nor height, nor depth, nor any other
creation, shall be able to separate us from
the love of God, which is in Christ Jesus,
our Lord.

Romans 8:38-39

EXAMINATION
Lord,
I'm afraid
    of this exam.
My brain
    is crammed
But recall
    is defective.
Can You restore
    a failing memory?

But the Comforter, who is the Holy Spirit,
whom the Father will send in my name, he
shall teach you all things, and bring all
things to your remembrance...
                John 14:26

INTERVIEW

Lord,
I'm afraid
of this interview.
Judgment
by another
rattles me.
So much at stake.
What if I don't
measure up?

And we know that all things work together
for good to them that love God, to them
who are the called according to his purpose.
Romans 8:28

TEMPER

Lord,
I'm afraid
    I'll lose my temper.
Patience
    is not my virtue.
Explosions
    are destructive
And my family
    is famous
    for short fuses.
Can You help me
    avoid a "blowup"?

But the fruit of the Spirit is love, joy, peace,
long-suffering, gentleness, goodness, faith,
meekness, self-control...
                Galatians 5:22-23

PRAYER

Lord,
I'm afraid
    to pray.
Others pray so well.
Polished
Professional
Pleasing to hear.
Must I sound pious
When I talk to You?

Be not ye, therefore, like unto them; for
your Father knoweth what things ye have
need of, before ye ask him.

Matthew 6:8

STANDING

Lord,
I'm afraid
    to take a stand.
Pliable
    is my name.
Going along
    I get along.
Is it really necessary
    to draw the line
    and make enemies?

Wherefore, take unto you the whole armor
of God, that ye may be able to withstand in
the evil day, and having done all, to stand.
Ephesians 6:13

EARTHQUAKES
Lord,
I'm afraid
of earthquakes.
Tremors
cause trembling.
The fault
must be
in me.
Is there anything
unshakable?

God is our refuge and strength, a very
present help in trouble. Therefore will not
we fear, though the earth be removed, and
though the mountains be carried into the
midst of the sea.

Psalm 46:1-2

SPEAKING UP

Lord,
I'm afraid
     to speak up.
Standards are falling.
Relative
     is the word.
Absolutes
     abandoned.
Is a silent witness
          sufficient
               in troubled times?

Cry aloud, spare not, lift up thy voice like a
trumpet, and show my people their
transgression, and the house of Jacob their
sins.

          Isaiah 58:1

NERVOUS BREAKDOWN
Lord,
I'm afraid
I'll break down.
Tears
are at floodtide
And the lump
in my throat
won't go away.
What works
at the breaking point?

Be still, and know that I am God....
Psalm 46:10
Cast thy burden upon the LORD, and he
shall sustain thee; he shall never suffer the
righteous to be moved.
Psalm 55:22

LOSS OF MIND

Lord,
I'm afraid
    I'll lose my mind.
The pressure
    seems unbearable.
Trifles
    masquerade
    as tragedies.
I feel like exploding.
Is mental health
    Your field?

For God hath not given us the spirit of fear,
but of power, and of love, and of a sound
mind.

                    2 Timothy 1:7

HOLDING OUT

Lord,
I'm afraid
    I can't hold out.
Why start
    when finishing
        is uncertain?
Hypocrisy
    disgusts me.
If I begin
    in faith
    will I fall?

Now unto him that is able to keep you from
falling, and to present you faultless before
the presence of his glory with exceeding
joy....

                        Jude 24

OTHER RACES

Lord,
I'm afraid
   of other races.
Can they be trusted?
Are they inferior?
Will they be in heaven?
Are they dangerous?
Shall I associate with them?
Are they important to You?

God, who made the world and all things in
it, seeing that he is Lord of heaven and
earth, dwelleth not in temples made with
hands...and hath made of one blood all
nations of men to dwell on all the face of
the earth....

Acts 17:24, 26

MINISTERS

Lord,
I'm afraid
of ministers.
Their piety
brings anxiety.
In their presence
I'm uncomfortable
self-conscious
ill-at-ease.
Are ministers divine?

And as Peter was coming in, Cornelius met
him, and fell down at his feet, and
worshiped him. But Peter took him up,
saying, Stand up; I myself also am a man.
Acts 10:25-26

WEEPING

Lord,
I'm afraid
    to weep.
Strength
    insists on silence.
Faith
    demands a front.
Inside
    I'm sobbing.
Are tears
    a sign of weakness?

Jesus wept.

John 11:35

THE MINISTRY

Lord,
I'm afraid
    to enter the ministry.
The call is certain
    but I'm not.
Can I live by faith?
Can I always love?
Will I stay compassionate?
Will I be faithful?
Am I willing to sacrifice?
Am I up to the task?

Not that we are sufficient of ourselves to
think anything as of ourselves, but our
sufficiency is of God.
                    2 Corinthians 3:5

ACCEPTING OFFICE
Lord,
I'm afraid
    to accept an office.
Nominations
    are numerous
But the thought of failure
        moves me to decline.
If I accept
    will I be wise enough
        to serve well?

If any of you lack wisdom, let him ask of
God, who giveth to all men liberally, and
upbraideth not, and it shall be given him.
James 1:5

THE BOSS

Lord,
I'm afraid
of my boss.
My future
belongs to him.
And he's unfriendly.
If I'm fired
will I survive?

The fear of man bringeth a snare; but whoso
putteth his trust in the LORD shall be safe.
Proverbs 29:25

RIDICULE

Lord,
I'm afraid
of ridicule.
So many things
I'd like
to attempt
But failure
invites
embarrassment.
Have You a promise
for sensitive souls?

Fear not; for thou shalt not be ashamed,
neither be thou confounded; for thou shalt
not be put to shame.

Isaiah 54:4

PERSECUTION

Lord,
I'm afraid
of persecution.
Martyrdom
is for missionaries.
Is it all right
to ease through life
Quietly
Offending nobody?

Yea, and all that will live godly in Christ
Jesus shall suffer persecution.
2 Timothy 3:12
Blessed are ye, when men shall revile you,
and persecute you, and shall say all manner
of evil against you falsely, for my sake.
Matthew 5:11

WRITING

Lord,
I'm afraid
    to write.
The prospect
    of editorial inspection
        paralyzes my pen.
And why write
    unless
        there are readers?
Can You find a publisher
        for my work?

The Lord gave the word; great was the
company of those who published it.
                    Psalm 68:11

VISITATION

Lord,
I'm afraid
    to do visitation.
Doorbells are disturbing.
I stand there
    regretting my ring
    hoping for no response
    dreading an open door.
Why should I visit?
Isn't the church
    for ministering?

And how I kept back nothing that was
profitable unto you, but have shown you,
and have taught you publicly, and from
house to house.

Acts 20:20

SURGERY

Lord,
I'm afraid
    to have surgery.
Anesthesia
    is a deep sleep
    and you wake up
    with parts missing.
Is it right
    to alter
        Your temple?

And the LORD God caused a deep sleep to
fall upon Adam, and he slept: and he took
one of his ribs, and closed up the flesh
instead thereof; and the rib, which the
LORD God had taken from man, made he a
woman, and brought her unto the man.

Genesis 2:21-22

PRISON

Lord,
I'm afraid
    to go to prison.
Tales told
    are incredible.
It's a jungle.
Can a praying prisoner
    expect maximum security?

The keeper of the prison looked not to
anything that was under his hand; because
the LORD was with him, and that which he
did, the LORD made it to prosper.

                      Genesis 39:23

FUNERALS

Lord,
I'm afraid
     to go to funerals.
Tears flow easily.
And what good
          is one more
               weeping guest?
Is grief-sharing
          important?

Rejoice with them that do rejoice, and weep
with them that weep.
Romans 12:15

WORLD DESTRUCTION
Lord,
I'm afraid
of total destruction.
Knowledge is exploding.
Will we?
Nuclear warheads
Hydrogen bombs
Germ warfare
Laser weapons
New life forms.
Is scientific suicide likely?

The LORD reigneth.

Psalm 97:1

CHILD'S DEATH
Lord,
I'm afraid
    I'll never see
    my child again.
I'm cried out.
Numb.
What hope remains
    when children die?

Can I bring him back again? I shall go to
him, but he shall not return to me.
2 Samuel 12:23

HOME TROUBLE

Lord,
I'm afraid
        my home
        is breaking up.
Barriers
        block communication.
Cold
        is the word.
What restores
        a failing marriage?

Wives, submit yourselves unto your own
husbands, as it is fit in the Lord. Husbands,
love your wives, and be not bitter against
them.

Colossians 3:18-19

DOUBTING GRACE
Lord,
I'm afraid
        it's too easy.
Believe,
        I'm told.
Trust,
And peace will come.
But it's too good
            to be true.
What about the law?
Ordinances?
Works?
What must I do
        to be saved?

Believe on the Lord Jesus Christ, and thou
shalt be saved, and thy house.
                                    Acts 16:31

WRONG DECISION
Lord,
I'm afraid
   I've made
   a wrong decision.
Hindsight nags.
Why didn't I?
What if?
Who would have thought?
How does one handle
   an irreversible blunder?

Forgetting those things which are behind,
and reaching forth unto those things which
are before, I press toward the mark for the
prize of the high calling of God in Christ
Jesus.

Philippians 3:13-14

EXPECTATIONS
Lord,
I'm afraid
    I'll fail others.
My best
    may not
    be good enough.
Letting people down
    is my specialty.
And expectations differ.
Whose opinion
    really counts?

And whatever ye do, do it heartily, as to the
Lord, and not unto men, knowing that of
the Lord ye shall receive the reward of the
inheritance; for ye serve the Lord Christ.
                    Colossians 3:23-24

HEIGHTS

Lord,
I'm afraid
   of heights.
A firm foundation
   is better
   than higher ground.
Fear climbs ladders
   rides elevators
   boards airplanes.
Mountaintop experiences
   are spiritual goals.
When I'm alarmed
   over altitude
   are You there?

If I ascend up into heaven, thou art there.
Psalm 139:8

CHILD'S SAFETY

Lord,
I'm afraid
for my child.
So many hazards
for little ones
And a parent
can't see
every danger.
Is anyone watching
when I'm not?

Take heed that ye despise not one of these
little ones; for I say unto you that in heaven
their angels do always behold the face of my
Father, who is in heaven.

Matthew 18:10

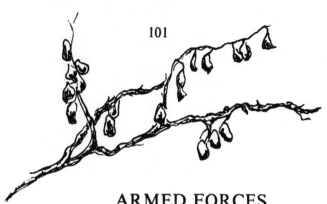

ARMED FORCES

Lord,
I'm afraid
to serve
as a soldier.
"Thou shalt not kill"
disarms me.
Is there a difference
between murder
and defending liberty?

To every thing there is a season, and a time
to every purpose under the heaven: A time
to love, and a time to hate; a time of war,
and a time of peace.

Ecclesiastes 3:1,8

ALONE
Lord,
I'm afraid
    to be alone.
Ticking clocks
    make melancholy moods.
Singing birds
    harmonize lonely tunes.
Silence
    intensifies
    isolation.
How can I feel secure
    when I'm alone?

Fear thou not; for I am with thee....
              Isaiah 41:10
For I, the LORD thy God, will hold thy
right hand, saying unto thee, Fear not; I will
help thee.
              Isaiah 41:13

GROUNDLESS FEARS
Lord,
I'm afraid
and I don't know why.
No storms threaten
But a cloud
hangs over me.
What shall I do
with this fear
of fear itself?

When I am afraid, I will trust in thee.
Psalm 56:3

MURPHY'S LAW

Lord,
I'm afraid
of Murphy's Law:
"Anything
that can go wrong
will go wrong."
Is that law
in Your Book?
Is failure
inevitable?
Are You against us?

The LORD is good to all: and his tender
mercies are over all his works.
Psalm 145:9

DROWNING

Lord,
I'm afraid
of drowning.
A youthful scare
affected me
to the depths.
Water's beauty
is for viewing
at a distance.
Boating
brings a sinking feeling.
Will you calm
my troubled seas?

And he saith unto them, Why are ye so
fearful, O ye of little faith? Then he arose,
and rebuked the wind, and the sea; and
there was a great calm.

Matthew 8:26

GIVING BIRTH
Lord,
I'm afraid
to give birth.
The vocabulary
of delivery
is disturbing.
Labor
Travail
Caesarean.
What is the effect
of the pain
of giving birth?

A woman, when she is in travail, hath
sorrow, because her hour is come; but as
soon as she is delivered of the child, she
remembereth no more the anguish, for joy
that a man is born into the world.
John 16:21

PASTOR LEAVING
Lord,
I'm afraid
   our pastor will leave.
"Discouraging"
   describes the response
      to his ministry.
But he's faithful.
And he loves us.
Will the church die
   if the pastor departs?

And he is before all things, and by him all
things consist. And he is the head of the
body, the church; who is the beginning, the
first-born from the dead, that in all things
he might have the pre-eminence.
                    Colossians 1:17-18

HUSBAND'S DEATH
Lord,
I'm afraid
     my husband will die.
And I need him.
Independence
     is today's word;
A strange goal
     for two
     that are one.
Must I achieve
     single security
     to be safe?

As I was with Moses, so I will be with thee;
I will not fail thee, nor forsake thee.
                    Joshua 1:5

WIFE'S DEATH
Lord,
I'm afraid
　　my wife will die.
"Together"
　　is another word
　　　　for happiness;
"Alone"
　　an expression
　　　　of despair.
Who'll walk with me
　　if I lose
　　the one I love?

And the LORD, he it is who doth go before
thee; he will be with thee, he will not fail
thee, neither forsake thee; fear not, neither
be dismayed.

Deuteronomy 31:8

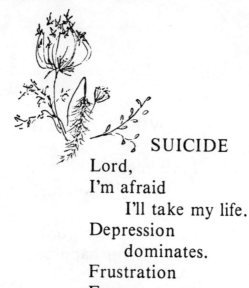

SUICIDE

Lord,
I'm afraid
    I'll take my life.
Depression
    dominates.
Frustration
Fear
Rejection
Despair
Are constant
    companions.
Is there a way out?

Come unto me, all ye that labor and are
heavy laden, and I will give you rest.
                    Matthew 11·28

GRIEF

Lord,
I'm afraid
    I'll not survive.
Friends
    stood with me.
The minister
    was kind.
Now it's over.
Everything
    is back to normal
Except me.
Do You have
    an encouraging word
    for a bewildered widow?

The LORD openeth the eyes of the blind; the
LORD raiseth those who are bowed down;
the LORD loveth the righteous; The LORD
preserveth the sojourners; he relieveth the
fatherless and widow.

Psalm 146:8-9

HOSPITALITY

Lord,
I'm afraid
  to be hospitable.
Entertaining
  calls for class.
Our home
  doesn't place
  in the parade.
And at feeding
  I'm less
  than best.
Why go out of the way
  when you can't
  go all the way?

Let love be without hypocrisy....Distributing
to the necessity of saints; given to
hospitality.

Romans 12:9,13

HOLIDAYS

Lord,
I'm afraid
of holidays.
Expectations
run high
But fall short.
And those
I long to see
don't show.
What can I do
to make holidays
happy?

Happy is that people whose God is the
LORD.

Psalm 144:15

Every day will I bless thee, and I will praise
thy name forever and ever.

Psalm 145:2

EMOTION

Lord,
I'm afraid
to show emotion.
Conservative
and controlled
are my words.
And I'm a man.
It's expected.
Sometimes
I feel
like shouting.
Would You mind?

And I beheld, and I heard the voice of many angels round about the throne and the living creatures and the elders, and the number of them was ten thousand times ten thousand, and thousands of thousands, saying with a loud voice, Worthy is the Lamb that was slain to receive power, and riches, and wisdom, and strength, and honor, and glory, and blessing.

Revelation 5:11-12

THE UNPARDONABLE SIN
　　　Lord,
　　I'm afraid
　　　　I've committed
　　　　the unpardonable sin.
　　Guilt
　　　　never leaves.
　　Conviction continues.
　　But I've waited so long
　　Knowing
　　　　of Your love.
　　Is there hope
　　　　for a sinner
　　　　　who wants
　　　　　to be saved?

All that the Father giveth me shall come to
me; and him that cometh to me I will in no
wise cast out.
　　　　　　　　　John 6:37

LEAVING HOME

Lord,
I'm afraid
   to leave home.
Freedom beckons.
Testing my wings
    appeals.
But security
    holds me.
Can I make it
    on my own?

Trust in the LORD, and do good; so shalt
thou dwell in the land, and verily thou shalt
be fed.

            Psalm 37:3

FORGOTTEN SIN

Lord,
I'm afraid
I've a sin
    unconfessed.
Something lurking.
Hidden.
But I don't know
    what it is.
Have I forgotten
    some evil act?
Will it rise
    in judgment?

I, the LORD, search the heart, I test the
conscience, even to give every man
according to his ways, and according to the
fruit of his doings.
Jeremiah 17:10

There is, therefore, now no condemnation to
them who are in Christ Jesus, who walk not
after the flesh, but after the Spirit.
Romans 8:1

THE ACCUSER
Lord,
I'm afraid
  I'm not forgiven
    completely.
Special sins
  of the past
  keep haunting.
Do You only forgive
    the easy ones?
If I'm forgiven
  who keeps resurrecting
    old regrets?

And I heard a loud voice saying in heaven,
Now is come salvation, and strength, and
the kingdom of our God, and the power of
his Christ; for the accuser of our brethren is
cast down, who accused them before our
God day and night.

Revelation 12:10

PEACE

Lord,
I'm afraid
    I'll never
    find peace.
Education
Success
Religion
Pills
Have promised
    and failed.
What's left?

Thou wilt keep him in perfect peace, whose
mind is stayed on thee, because he trusteth
in thee.

Isaiah 26:3

INDEX